The Angry Bear

An Aesop's Fable

Retold by Annette Smith

Illustrations by Pat Reynolds

It was spring.

A big brown bear
came out of his cave.
He had been asleep
all winter.

Now he was very hungry.

The bear walked
down to the river.

He wanted to get a fish.

A bee buzzed
around the bear's head.

The bear looked up
and the fish got away.

The bear was very angry and he ran after the bee.

The bee flew
into an old log
in the long grass.

The bear hit the log
with his big paws.

Lots of bees
came out of the log.

They buzzed around
and around
the bear's head.

The bear had to get away
very fast.

He ran back to the river
and jumped into the water.

The bees flew away,
and the bear
got a fish.

After that,

the bear never let the bees

make him angry again.